31

to a *Simple Life*
The *Amish Way*

Karen Anna Vogel

31 Days to a Simple Life the Amish Way:

Inspirational Secrets from Amish Friends

Lamb Books

Contact the author on Face book at:
www.facebook.com/VogelReaders

Learn more the author at: www.karenannavogel.com

Visit her blog, Amish Crossings, at
www.karenannavogel.blogspot.com

~Dedication~
To my grandchildren,
my precious ones.

Introduction

After thirty years, I'm still gleaning secrets to a simpler life from Amish friends. I was afraid of them at first, thinking they were stoic, judgmental people. Maybe it was the drab black and blue outfits worn by the Troyer Amish in Western New York. Their curtains were navy blue and well, they certainly didn't seem welcoming. After getting to know a few families, I can see why "off the gridders" to Spiritual enthusiasts are flocking to them for plain and simple advice. Seven million people visit Lancaster County alone every year, and that's just one county. Amish are now in 40-some states, so it's likely if you live in the USA or Canada, you may drive to a settlement and meet a few Amish.

We'll explore a suggestion written in *The Budget*, an Amish newspaper.

"A common question now in America. How can I become Amish? Answer: If you admire our faith, strengthen yours. If you admire our sense of commitment, deepen yours. If you admire our community spirit, build your own. If you admire the simple life, cut back. If you admire deep character and enduring values, live them yourself."

The Amish live intentionally, as their many proverbs about time well spent, either on a project or figuring out a problem mentally.

"Regrets over yesterday and the fear of tomorrow are twin thieves that rob us of the moment."

The years can fly past like a flock of geese.

Live each short hour with God and the long years will take care of themselves'

Both of my parents were first generation immigrants. My mom passed on some Italian sayings and my dad his Croatian. When I was a teen I was shocked to find that "cleanliness is next to godliness" and "charity begins at home" were not in the Bible. I checked "If you can't say anything nice, don't say anything at all' was in there, and it's not either.

So, I do understand the Amish with their sayings. They're taught to their children as little nibbles of wisdom to steer them in life.

This book isn't about Amish sayings, but they'll be riddled throughout, so you can better understand their thinking.

You can skip around this book, starting on day 20 if you like. If it's a day you're snowed in, you may want to spend some time decluttering the home.

I'm so blessed to have learned so much from the Amish. I hope you'll be inspired as you read this book, finding a path a bit less chaotic.

Day 1
If you admire our faith,
strengthen yours

"How much does it cost for a cord of split wood, Harry?" I asked my paraplegic Amish friend.

"I don't know. The People fill my woodshed every year," he said, gratitude etched into his face.

Harry's story is not uncommon. I've seen the effects of the Amish slower paced life; they have time to value what's really important: faith, family, and friends.

MIT Technology Review wrote in their *Technology and Happiness* article:

There is, though, one group of Americans that is imperturbably sunny: the Amish. Their depression rates are negligibly low relative to the rest of society. Their happiness levels are consistently high. The Pennsylvania Amish, when asked how much they agree with the statement: You are satisfied with your life (using a scale of 1 to 10), turn out to be as happy as the members of the Forbes 400.

I wasn't surprised that the Amish are as satisfied as the 400 richest Americans. I told Amish friends about this article, and they just shrug and throw out a proverb like: "He who has no money is poor; he who has nothing but money is even poorer." They value strong family ties, life-long friendships and a faith that permeates everything.

When I drive around Amish country, I see small *dawdyhaus* (grandparent houses) built next to the main farmhouses. Amish place such high regard on the family, but the care towards aging parents is a such a proven track record, they're exempt from paying social security! The People's care for their elderly is their security. If the aging parent suffers from any impairment, they take care of them in the home. My friend in Smicksburg told me a stroke patient, who was paralyzed, was taken care of around the clock by family.

Friendships in America are at an all-time low. Duke University's *Social Isolation in America* study found that people have fewer friends outside of their immediate family, due to long work hours. Internet friendships have also replaced face-to-face communication, and people are feeling more alone than ever. The Amish, by contrast know the importance of friendship. When someone dies, they can expect to be visited by friends weekly for a year, until their grief subsides. I find this amazing.

The Amish are a branch of Christianity that tries to live out the words of Jesus, especially the Sermon on the Mount found in the Bible, Matthew 5-7. It can be broken down into five categories. The first is the Beatitudes, blessings to comfort believers, such as "*Blessed are the merciful, for they shall obtain mercy,*" and "*Blessed are the meek, for they shall inherit the earth.*" The second category is New Laws, such as going the extra mile and loving your neighbor. The third category is the Lord's Prayer, or the Our Father, as some people call it. The fourth is about the dangers of the love of money, and the fifth is a warning to be wise verses foolish.

I'm challenged by this in many areas. Turn off Facebook and visit people face to face. Our family has decided to have Sunday dinners again, and I'm reading Matthew 5-7 a lot more, seeing how I can put feet to my faith.

Day 2
If you admire our sense of commitment, deepen yours.

Most people see Amish one-day barn raisings as the epitome of commitment, which it is. Someone in the community has the action plan and everyone knows what size nails, lumber, tools and whatnot to bring. There's a date set and Amish travel from miles around, but mostly it's the people in their church district who do the work. But how do you take this level of commitment and apply it to your everyday life?

Think of a benefit dinner. We'll be going to one next month for someone who lost everything in a house fire. Because this family has community, many are reaching out, buying clothes and other essentials.

But if you're living outside of a community of some sorts, you're isolated and your needs aren't known. The local church mirrors the Amish more than anything. Church steeples could be seen when entering a town long ago as a safe place for a traveler to get help while in distress. Churches weren't mega either and neither are Amish church districts. Their maximum number is two-hundred. They create a new district when that number is met.

You can find community outside the church as well, but finding time is the biggest hindrance. I know what the Amish say. "You make time for what's important."

We've changed our lives by the Amish example of 'Don't put off until tomorrow what you can do today'. In other words, be pro-active. So, we were going to a big church and feeling not too connected. We now attend a small church with less than two-hundred people, and it's more conducive to a tight-knit community.

The Amish have dinner together on their 'Off-Sundays'. They only have a church service every other week. On the Off-Sundays, they're encouraged to fellowship over a meal. So, we're trying to be more pro-active in this area.

Eating a meal with someone is time spent together and naturally bonds are formed. Hospitals got their name from hospitality. *Hmm.* Seems like we're to invite not only our best friends but people who may be in need.

Ecclesiastes 4:12 says:

A person standing alone can be attacked and defeated, but two can stand back-to-back and conquer. Three are even better, for a triple-braided cord is not easily broken.

So, to fight against isolation, join hands with others. It's the Amish way.

Day 3
If you admire our community spirit, build your own

The Amish community is strong, even though they're very busy people working long hours. They incorporate work with fellowship. Work and frolic don't seem to fit together. It's like saying, 'work festival'. But this is how they kill two birds with one stone. They combine work with fun. For example, if a family builds a new house and the inside needs painted, they get together and paint and have fun talking as they work.

Quilting bees are the most commonly known work frolic, but there are many others. Canning, baking, shelling peas.... it's endless, really. Anything that can be done together to make the burden lighter and to have fun can be made into a frolic.

I visited an Amish friend last week and saw something very unique. A group of ten men were cutting ice blocks from a pond and hauling them to an icehouse on a huge wagon, pulled by draft horses. They paused to talk, laugh and sing. *Yes, sing.* The Amish sing when they work. When they replaced the roof on our house they were up there singing in German.

Besides work frolics, the Amish make holidays. One I'd like to see in the English world is Sister Day. I have two sisters and our relationships need to be celebrated. We do on birthdays, but to have one day a year to really reflect on what sisterhood really means and to plan how to strengthen our ties would be awesome.

The Amish also have three Christmas dates: Dec. 25th, 26th and Jan. 6th. They don't buy expensive presents, but have a feast similar to our Thanksgiving meal.

In our busy world, we could learn from the Amish and either have work frolics or special holidays. My garden is always too big, so instead of trying to pick all the produce ourselves, we invite family and friends over at harvest time. Something my daughters and I started was Girls Only Weekend. My husband and son created Guys Only Weekend." My sister's having a Christmas party in May!

Day 4
If you admire the simple life, cut back

The "Small House Movement" amazes me. People are living in not small, but tiny houses, some only 300 square feet. They claim they've never been happier and I believe them. The MacMansions of the 1980's are not in vogue anymore, since people are realizing they were working quite hard for a status symbol, but were slaves to their jobs. Books like *Not So Big House* and *Not so big Remodeling* by Sarah Susanka really freed up my husband and me when we remodeled our 1897 farmhouse. We could have put on a giant sized addition, but we decided on a modest one. We didn't realize just how keeping up with the Jones's was ingrained in our thinking.

One of my favorite Amish men, Noah, from Smicksburg, helped build our addition. One day when I went to pick him up for work, I was quite surprised that he had switched houses with another relative. He said they needed a bigger house, so they switched.

Talk about holding all things lightly! So here my husband and I sit with a three-bedroom house of medium size, and my daughter and her husband are looking for a house to raise a family. Should we sell them our house and build a small one in the back of our two acres, like the Amish do? I am always challenged by these people.

Author Richard J Foster, says: "We really must understand that the lust for affluence in contemporary society is psychotic. It is psychotic because it has completely lost touch with reality. We crave things we neither need nor enjoy. 'We buy things we do not want to impress people we do not like.' ...It is time to awaken to the fact that conformity to a sick society is to be sick." (*Celebration of Discipline: The Path to Spiritual Growth*)

Cutting back can also mean getting rid of things that clutter our time. Television is a big time stealer along with video games. In this area, we're almost Amish. We like relational activities like playing cards, visiting and board games. When I first got to know the Amish, I asked them bluntly, "How do you live without television? I'd die!" Miriam Hershberger's face lit up. "Raising white pigeons, bird watching, astronomy, reading, quilting, visiting, sledding...." Her list went on, and I felt sad. She was really living, and I was wasting my life through television. I decided then to cut back. Ten years later, we only watch shows online. You can watch most anything live-streamed these days, and watch it when you like.

I'm always on a quest to cut back on "trifles" as William Penn called them...things that just take our time and have no meaning.

Day 5
If you admire deep character and enduring values, live them yourself

Sometimes I envy the Amish. They're adamant about eating together and sharing family stories passed down through the generations. Well, it takes me back to Italy and visiting my cousins and all the food and stories. I miss them, but am trying to bring the tradition back home.

When we hired Amish crews to put on our new roof, addition and a barn, we always saw how they'd get fidgety at 3:30 pm. "Need to get home in time for dinner," they'd gasp. "Wife doesn't like it if we're late." I turned around and laughed; such masculine men worried if they'd get a tongue lashing if late.

Ray, who has nine children told me as I drove them home, that eating together was a high priority. "I see the *kinner* and my wife. We eat at 4:00 pm every day." I wondered why it was written in stone and he said it gave ample time to not only eat (and an Amish meal isn't complete without a dessert) but "It keeps us close," he said.

You can Google "Bonding over food", "Family meal times" to find the benefits of eating regularly together. But what the Amish do is share stories after dinner, or read from the Bible or Martyr's Mirror. They are fed spiritually now and get to their roots. The Martyr's Mirror's full name describes it well: *The Bloody Theater or Martyrs Mirror of the Defenseless Christians who baptized only upon confession of faith, and who suffered and died for the testimony of Jesus, their Saviour, from the time of Christ to the year A.D. 1660.*

So, Amish families are reminded daily that when non-Amish gawk or tease them, accuse them of anything from animal cruelty to being a cult, they're not shocked. They have a sense of perspective. For hundreds of years the Amish have been misunderstood to the point of death, so they don't expect to fit in.

This bonding time can be made in any home. My husband and I eat together, the kids having flown the coop, and we pray and talk about our concerns and joys. We call it our daily 'pow wow'. This sweet pause in the day to cook for each other is precious. It's a gift to have one human being really care to hear the daily updates on my life.

Day 6
The Serenity Prayer

I'm taking my sister-in-law to the hospital today for things she needs to get done for her kidney transplant. I love Suzanne so much and am afraid of losing her. So I say the Serenity Prayer. It's a longer prayer than people think. The Amish have adopted this prayer and others. The Serenity Prayer was written by Pastor Reinhold Niebuhr in 1934, during the Great Depression.

This prayer covers all areas of life and has been adopted by Alcoholics Anonymous and other Twelve Step programs. I'll be using it today...maybe you will too.

Here's the whole prayer:

God grant me the serenity to accept the things I cannot change;

Courage to change the things I can; and wisdom to know the difference.

Living one day at a time; enjoying one moment at a time;

Accepting hardships as the pathway to peace;

Taking, as He did, this sinful world as it is, not as I would have it;

Trusting that He will make all things right if I surrender to His will;

That I may be reasonably happy in this life and supremely happy with Him

Forever in the next.

Amen.

The first prayer an Amish child will learn is *The Lord's Prayer*. It's said every day in Amish schools, even though religion is not, as parents are expected to teach them about Christianity in the home.

Prayers handed down from their ancestors from the 1700's is now in English. It's simply called *The Devoted Christian Prayer Book* and can be purchased for $4.99 from Pathway Publishers. It's a hardcover well-bound book. So cheap you'd think it would be a paperback, but like the Amish always say, "We don't believe in extortion."

Day 7
Downsize

The Amish have helped us remodel and add on to our little farmhouse for several years. They questioned why we were adding on, since our kids were grown. "They're never leaving," we replied. "Four young adults in their 20s with no spouses and not much hope."

Well, I believe God has a sense of humor, because we're having our third wedding in two years and another in June. So, all four of our kids will have gotten married in three years.

So, we have a big house for just Tim and me. I have to say, we love it. But as I was writing *Knit Together: An Amish Knitting Novel,* that is very semiautobiographical, we downsize, like Ginny and James. Well, we just did too, and moved into our *"dawdyhaus"* or grandparent house.

The Amish take care of their aging parents in small houses either attached to the main house or built separately. They are adorable, plain and simple. Tim and I are also fascinated with the Tiny House Movement, where people are living in 300 square feet. It seems rather liberating and cozy.

About our new *'dawdyhaus'.* When Tim and I went to a fantastic B&B last fall, a plan started to evolve in our minds. They have a common room, with couches and tables, and then the kitchen which was self-serve, and bedrooms. *Why don't we do this with our son and daughter-in-law? We'd have built in housecleaners.* (We call them Mr. & Mrs. Clean) I was so sick of cleaning a big old farmhouse, and since the house isn't an open floor plan and very long, we could section things off.

We'll we did it. Tim and I now have four rooms: bedroom, living room, little "parlor" room, bath and laundry. Our son and daughter-in-law have the rest of the house, and we have a middle room we share in common, that we call The Commons. We share the kitchen but eat in different areas, needing space and well defined boundaries. Tim and I eat in a little sunroom off the kitchen, and they eat in The Commons.

I recently saw on YouTube a plan for multigenerational living. Contractors are having a hard time selling McMansions, so they're offering houses for three generations! The reason customers are choosing to purchase are built-in babysitters and college age kids living at home so they can commute to college, making it affordable.

Our reasons for living in a little *dawdyhaus* are that our kids were raised to not be in debt. My son and daughter-in-law can save money and pay cash for a home in a few years. When they leave, we can let another one of our kids take their place or help a family in need. We also like the coziness of it all.

I feel like I live in a B&B every day, now. Mr. and Mrs. Clean keep the kitchen and The Commons sparkling clean.

Day 8
Organized bliss

It wasn't long ago that every woman knew the saying:

Monday: Wash Day
Tuesday: Ironing Day
Wednesday: Sewing Day
Thursday: Market Day
Friday: Cleaning Day
Saturday: Baking Day
Sunday: Day of Rest

Not only Laura Ingalls Wilder knew this; my mother and other ladies said it when I was a kid running around the neighborhood in the 1960's. But when I go to Amish country, I do see laundry hung on Mondays.

I asked my friend, Barb, mother of nine, how she washes her clothes. She said they use boiling water in a large pot and 'swoosh' the clothes around. I immediately thought of my grandma who came from rural Italy. She washed clothes the same way, and when she got a wringer washer, it was her emancipation day.

Most Amish use wringer washers. But as I sat in Barb's house asking her about laundry day, she was very relaxed. Her teenage daughters were boiling water to wash dishes. They added to the conversation, since they did a lot of the laundry. Once again, I'm taken back. They have such willingness and cheerfulness about work. I know women who are still washing their college age "kids" clothes.

So, when you go into Amish country and see the lines of laundry, don't think there's one tired Amish mom in there doing it all. It's a group activity and by the responses of other Amish women, something not dreaded. They do admit they don't like hanging clothes in the winter. Yes, they hang them year round. The clothes are 'freeze-dried'.

Another thing that amazes me is how clean they keep their clothes. When Amish men worked on our house, I have to admit, I didn't drive them home unless *all* the windows were

21

down. The odor of "hard work" was upon them, and I couldn't breathe. But these same clothes were worn again and they smelled zestfully clean. I give Amish women of all ages a lot of credit for taking care of the men's work clothes.

Day 9

Read Amish books and magazines

Even though I've known Amish folks for years, when I wrote *Knit Together*, I went to the source of the spring: books written by the Amish. I wanted to read for myself what baptismal candidates had to study before I had my English character, Joseph, contemplate being Amish. My literary agent laughed at my concern for Joseph, reminding me he wasn't real. But to me, he was, and had a strong walk with God. If he turned Amish, would he be bound by laws of man that only kill? I was surprised at how rich, inspirational, yet challenging, these books were to my faith.

I bought *The Dordrecht Confession of Faith* for a dollar. One dollar. Since I was paying shipping, I figured I should get my bulk-rate worth. So I added to my chart, *Devoted Christian's Prayer Book,* which is a hardcover book which includes *Rules of a Godly Life,* which consists of forty-seven proverbs. (Included in the back of this book). I couldn't resist buying *1001 Questions and Answers on the Christian Life,* just to see what questions people not familiar with the Amish would ask… to my shock, I learned a lot!

Then I saw that they had magazines! I love magazines, so I paid a year's subscription to *Family Life.* Their blurb reads:

It contains articles on Christian living, parenting, and homemaking. It also contains editorials, letters from readers, medical advice, poems, recipes, and children's stories.

To date, this magazine is my favorite, even topping *Country Living.* It really gives you an inside look into an Amish home. An article written by an Amish woman called, "I Married Money", told of her husband's addiction to work, keeping up appearances with Amish neighbors, and never being satisfied with what he had. It was a strong warning to unmarried women, since she felt there were hints of his love of money during their courtship.

Since I homeschooled my four kids, I was familiar with Pathway Publishing and Christian Light Publications. We used the Mennonite curriculum by CLP and my kids all read the *Pathway Readers*, books used in Amish schools. We lived by the Amish and thought it would be a 'novel' idea at first, but then *I* got hooked on Pathway Readers.

All the books mentioned can be bought online at Pathway Publishing. It's run by the English, and I'm so glad. You used to have to write a check and order snail mail to Canada. Visit http://pathway-publishers.com or Christian Light Publications at http://www.clp.org. I guarantee that once you start reading books or magazine written by the Amish, you'll get the best education about their ways.

You can also buy historical fiction. A favorite author among the Amish and Mennonites is Christmas Carol Kaufman. *Not Regina* is not only well-written, but tells of the persecution of the Anabaptists.

Day 10
Daddy time

Think of *Little House on the Prairie* and *The Walton's* TV shows where both fathers stayed at home or near home, always accessible to his family. This is the Amish view of fatherhood. Men stay home and work like the Pre-Industrial Revolution Era. Farming meets this need, but so do many other small family businesses.

Fathers having to leave the home to work for the English is one of their biggest challenges to date. I know an Amish family of nine children ranging in age from a wee baby to teenagers. They did everything they could to keep dad at home. He walks down the road to work at a sawmill part-time, they have two large greenhouses, and the oldest daughter is a schoolteacher, adding her pay to the family money pot. But they aren't making it and Abe got a 9-5 job away from home. They are visibly grieved by this.

Amish fathers typically take care of the animals and farm chores. They plow and plant their fields, even if it's only a few acres. They eke out a living by many means, by selling sweet corn, vegetables from their garden. Basically, they do everything they can to keep dad at home. But why?

Well, they take seriously scriptures in Deuteronomy:

You shall love the Lord your God with all your heart and with all your soul and with all your might. And these words that I command you today shall be on your heart. You shall teach them diligently to your children, and shall talk of them when you sit in your house, and when you walk by the way, and when you lie down, and when you rise."

So, you don't sit down little Johnny and give him a list of rules to memorize. Most things are caught, not taught. So, a father living out the Christian life in front of his children is a constant object lesson.

Also, there are conversations that just pop up. Maybe a father and his daughter are out in the barn and she has something on her mind: a problem. The father senses this and asks her what's wrong and she spills the beans. These are called the 'teachable moments' that aren't planned or scheduled. A father will miss them if he's off to work. Dad can't sit his children down at the end of the day and ask them to pour out their hearts. It flows out naturally, trickle by trickle throughout the day. Amish families want to be the ones who instill Godly living in their children. They don't even want the Bible taught in their one-room schoolhouses. No, this is the responsibility of the parents, especially the fathers.

Many Amish families forego the extras of life to keep dad at home. He's their valued teacher and helper in life, not just a hard worker who provides a paycheck. He's Pa Ingalls wiping Laura's tears because Almanzo isn't paying attention to her. He's Mr. Walton who works by his sons giving advice when asked. He's home and home is where the heart is.

Day 11
Garden

Gardening is a way of showing that you believe in tomorrow.

I used to tell people to get to know an Amish woman, just ask her for a recipe, but

I'd ask for garden seeds or catalogs, too. You see, Amish have gardens of all sizes, and most find pleasure spending time in them.

The kitchen garden is right off their kitchens. You can run out and get some basics for a salad or herbs or other greens used in a recipe. It's close enough too, to go outside and pull a carrot and munch. It's like their outdoor refrigerator for many months. Early spring in Pennsylvania can bring a bumper crop of peas and other 'early' vegetables. The season is extended into the fall by growing hardy kale, spinach, broccoli and other 'late' crops.

We have a kitchen garden, but it's all in containers with groundcover all around. It's part of the landscaping of our farmhouse. Some Amish grow herbs along their homes for décor, dill looking amazingly lovely.

Amish women are 'proud in a *goot* way' about their flower gardens. They not only line their homes with brilliant colors, but have round patches lined with field stones. One Amish friend has her stones painted white. I asked her why and she just stared at her flowers fondly. "I think it looks prettier." No deep meaning, just something she takes pleasure in.

Many find emotional and physical healing in gardening. I have two friends who are crazy about flowers. I used to say, "If you can't eat it, it's taking up space." Sigh, I do need to lighten up. So, these friends inspired me to plant bulbs in hues of purple and yellow all along our sidewalk leading to the mailbox. I feel like a kid seeing them right now coming up! Actually, I think deep down, my massacre of indoor plants has made me feel like a failure. (If you can't keep a cactus alive, hang it up!)

Plants show there are seasons in life. The Amish seem to have a better grip on the length of life at a younger age. It's almost foreign to the American way of thinking. When autumn comes and flowers dry up, they collect seeds for next year. It teaches patience and gives hope. That little dead marigold seed houses thousands of little baby seeds and next spring, they can be 'born again'.

The Secret Garden book enchants me. You can see that Mary, Mary, quite contrary and her invalid cousin literally bloom the more the garden is nurtured. A passage from this book pricks me:

Much more surprising things can happen to anyone who, when a disagreeable or discouraged thought comes into his mind, just has the sense to remember in time and push it out by putting in an agreeable, determinedly courageous one. Two things cannot be in one places

"Where you tend a rose my lad, a thistle cannot grow."

As I write this, I have some thorns (stressors) I can do nothing about. I'm giving myself permission to putter in the garden, even if it's not a vegetable 'earning its keep'. I'm watching my spring bulbs bloom and it's so serene. Maybe I'll try planting some perennials around our pond.

Day 12

Gelassenheit: serenity in quietly waiting

I treasure this trait among the Amish more than anything. *Gelassenheit* is putting others first, the Golden Rule seen in technicolor among the Amish. When speaking in a group, all eyes are upon you, taking in every word said, and then you may find the 'Amish pause'. They take to heart what you've said and want to give you their full attentive answer.

For example, I asked a man named Levi about what he thought of Old Order Amish verses New Order Amish. He bowed his head, pulled at his beard and said nothing. I thought I'd pushed it this time, asking too many questions or touched a nerve. After a 'spell', Levi kindly looked up and said, "I think an older Amish person can explain it better. They're wiser than I am."

I almost fainted. Here he was, in his prime at thirty-some years old and he's saying he doesn't know it all, that the older the wiser and he meant it.

Gelassenheit is seen in their culture through their personality, yet they have nicknames like 'Tall Laughing Jonah'. Some are hilarious to talk to, but there's still that deep down seriousness that comes with being an attentive listener. And if you say something you shouldn't, they usually just smile, overlooking quickly any hurt or irritation. Talking to Barb, mother of nine, I blurted out, "Oh my goodness you put up the hard way. Have you heard of a vacuum sealer?" Silence and then a smirk from Barb. Her daughters were there and I may have enticed them to dream of greener pastures. Without having to be told to stop tempting her daughters with modern gadgets needing electricity, I got the message. I simply said, "But to each their own, I suppose. Many can with a pressure cooker and love it."

Gelassenheit in German means 'serenity'. In the Amish Froschauer (German) Bible they take this virtue from Lamentations 3:26 and it means 'quietly wait'. So, when I flubbed up in front of Barb's daughters, she was quietly waiting for me to get the cue to say the right thing: don't tempt my daughters to go the English route.

Gelassenheit is part of the Amish *Ordnung*, which is German for order. This serenity or quietly waiting is shown in their simplicity of clothing, house style and having things in common. No competition to keep up with the Schmuckers.

This is not to say that they've lost their identity, as so many are known for their unique talents, but their hope is that it all points to their simple lifestyle. By putting others first, Amish businesses don't believe in 'extortion'. They say that right out loud. "Why should we charge you too much if we're happy with our profit." Again, you just want to hold on to a chair, shocked.

My good friend, Maryann, had to get her entire kitchen replaced due to flooding. She shopped around and was discouraged. Since we go to Smicksburg often, we thought of Amish cabinet and furniture makers. and you they don't cut corners. (No pun intended) They use real hardwoods and are upfront about costs. They have a yearlong waiting list because Maryann got a custom-made kitchen with over twenty cabinets plus an island as big as a dining room table, installed, for $12,000.00. Let me spell that out if you missed it: twelve-thousand dollars. And her cabinets are cherry!

So how can we embrace this 'serenity'? For me it's jumping out of our performance based culture. What you achieve isn't more important than who you are. Having the biggest house on the block doesn't mean it's the happiest one. Finding joy in serving others is what's important. An Amish proverb, painted on a simple little board, lives on my kitchen window sill. "The most important things are not things." It brings serenity to my soul every time I wash dishes.

Day 13
Volunteer

Can you picture a group of Amish men flying cows into Romania to start a farm to feed orphans? How about Amish distributing Bibles door to door? How about Amish women processing 400,000 cans of chicken, beef and hamburger to give to the needy? The latter seems Amish, doesn't it? We see the Amish as folk living quaint lives on the farm. Let me help blow your mind!

Christian Aid Ministries (CAM) is a worldwide Amish and Mennonite charitable organization run by volunteers that log in over 200,000 hours of work a year. The ministry receives nearly $134 million in donations, ranking near well-known ministries such as Samaritans Purse ($150 million) and Christian Children's Fund ($133 million). Incredibly, 97.4% of this money actually goes toward relief efforts in the US and around the world. (Some charitable organizations give less than 70% to their actual cause). CAM has staff, bases and distribution networks in Romania, Moldova, Ukraine, Haiti, Nicaragua, Liberia and Israel. I was blown away completely. CAM is doing a top-notch job.

So what is CAM doing right now? According to their newsletter, their international focus is the Ebola crisis in Africa and Syrian refuge relief.

Food-Parcels-For-Syrian-Refugees

Since the civil war in Syria began in 2011, hundreds of thousands have died, and millions have been forced to flee their homes. These refugees gather in meager refugee camps, struggling to provide food, shelter, and clothing for their families. Winter storms sweeping the Middle East leave many refugees vulnerable to the elements.

Through sponsors like you, Syrian refugees in the Middle East will be able to rely on a monthly source of food and other basic supplies. The stress of providing for their families in a foreign environment is eased by the compassion of CAM contacts delivering the aid.

Each $50 donation provides a Syrian family with a food parcel containing rice, beans, meat, and other nutritious items.

Here in the USA:

CAM's Rapid Response teams are designed to move into a community within twenty-four hours after a disaster strikes. They investigate damages and then bring cleanup volunteers into the area within forty-eight hours or less. Volunteers help cut up trees, install tarps on damaged roofs, and do other cleanup projects. The purpose of Rapid Response Services is to be a Christian testimony in the United States and demonstrate a faith that works: "…. faith without works is dead…" (James 2:20).

For more information on Christian Aid Ministries, visit their website, run by less conservative Mennonites who use electricity

and the internet.
http://www.christianaidministries.org

I've chosen to really spotlight CAM in my *Amish Knitting Circle Series*. The women in the circle knit warm items that are sent to Eastern Europe. In real life, my readers send scarves, hats, shawls, etc. to CAM and they ship them to Ukraine or Romania. I hope it will raise awareness for this wonderful ministry.

Day 14
Start a small business

The Amish have extraordinary savvy business skills. Some make a living by running two or three. My friend, Lydia, has two greenhouses and her husband built a bulk goods store across the street from their house for a source of income. What impresses me is how they agonize over getting the best prices so they can pass the savings on to customers who travel far to stock up, since their prices are *one-fourth* the average price.

Amish friends who are construction workers are excited about their new business making tiny houses. The Tiny House Movement is sweeping the USA. When they first found out that their competition was selling these little 300 square feet houses for $40,000.00 they gawked. I thought they were mentally counting money, but they weren't. They simply said, "We'll sell them much cheaper, at a fair price." So, *fair* pay and *fair* prices are at the core of an Amish work ethic.

My daughter ordered them a book on tiny house construction and floor plans, which includes sources to buy all necessary appliances. My daughter joked with them that they should get old-fashioned Ben Franklin pot belly stoves and make the interior look like an Amish house. At first we all laughed and then…light bulb. "What a great idea," Joe quipped.

My favorite businessman is Leander, who helps run Yoder's Antique Mall in Punxsutawney. He feels it's his 'gift'. This Old Order Amish man, reads marketing books all the time. "Oh, I love Dale Carnegie's book, *How to Win Friends and Influence People*, read it sixteen times last year. I love John Maxwell, too," Leander said. "I have a passion for running a business," he added. "It's my gift. I can't get enough of it." Leander travels to teach *Englishers* how to run businesses since the Amish are super entrepreneurial and outsiders want in on their secrets to success.

Whether it be running a vegetable stand, sell fudge at farmer's markets, grow herbs to sell for medicinal purposes or tiny shops selling baskets, quilts, crocheted or knit items, Amish rockers, Amish dolls etc. they're making a contribution.

Many Amish families, some quite large, live off of approximately $35,000 a year. They pay all taxes except social security since they have a proven record of taking care of their elderly. So making quilts for a price of 500 dollars apiece really adds to the family pie. They remind me of my mom when working as a shoe clerk during the Great Depression. She gave her pay check to her dad and they all contributed to the family finances.

I see great sense of accomplishment among Amish young people. They're free to work after eighth grade and they're more mature than many adults. I rarely hear them complain...

Day 15

Pare down the wardrobe

Okay, for starters, I don't wear a bonnet or dress plain. But I admit, I envy how Amish women can just get up in the morning and take an outfit off the peg and, *voila*, are dressed in no time. No wondering if clothes match, no tripping over the shoes left around the room.

I got the opportunity to visit France several years ago. I gaped at the women. All solid colored clothes with colorful scarves. Something clicked. After a week of talking to locals, I found that they don't have room for many things, living in small flats. They think Americans have too much of everything and make fun of us.

I was so taken by these women in France, as they dressed so stylish, but I needed more advice. I read an article, *Jamie Lee Curtis Comes Clean*, in *Good Housekeeping Magazine*. She opened her closet for the world to see, and it had blacks, navy blues, and whites. Jamie Lee said:

I have a rule: Pretend you're going on a trip for two weeks, and pull what you'd wear on that two-week trip, and get rid of everything else. Per season — like, you can do a winter trip. It's like, how many peacoats or jackets do you need? I have a navy blue one and a black one — done. I wear navy blue, black, and white; I'm not really a clothes person, but I know what looks good on me and what doesn't.

If she 'breaks' this rule she donates. *"I don't throw anything away — I give. There's no nicer feeling, ever."*

I'm writing about homelessness in the *Amish Knitting Circle Series*, and I just can't ignore my wasteful living anymore. So, I've taken the plunge to dress "plain". My closet is looking more like Jamie Lee Curtis's. I gave 2/3rds of my wardrobe to Salvation Army. This awesome ministry helps the homeless in many ways, so I thought it fitting. I have to say, I feel lighter somehow. It's taken me a few years to figure it out, so I thought I'd pass

the information on to you. Now…go get rid
of some shoes!

Day 16
Glean from people of all ages

Growing up in the 1960's, it was common
to go next door and chat with and checkup on
elderly neighbors. It was also common to
know everyone in the entire neighborhood of
fifty houses or more.

When Tim and I moved to New York in
the 80's we soon had four preschoolers and
intentionally got them involved with church,
the 'Granny' of the church always patiently
waiting while they told her of their
adventures. Meeting Amish families
underscored our beliefs that children thrived
socially in a multi-generational atmosphere,
and our decision to homeschool began.

When meeting a new Amish person, the
older kids always come to listen to our
conversations. I discovered that they were
being mentored, to learn how to speak to
people of all ages. They weren't shooed off to
mind their business, the world is their

schoolroom. Amish are asked tough questions by us Englishers, and the kids are learning how to respond with kindness yet firmness if necessary.

The one-room schoolhouse is from grades 1-8, the older ones helping the younger. Schools were like this until Henry Ford made cars accessible to the public, and soon school buses could transport children longer distances.

But this only happened in the 1920s, not long ago. So, children being segregated by age is relatively a new thing and the jury is still out on the pros and cons.

The elderly Amish I've met are as sharp as tacks. A ninety-year-old Amish woman chatted with me about the settlement she helped form and Amish beliefs for hours. The next time I visited, she was too busy to talk because she was sewing clothes for her many grandchildren.

A new phenomenon I hope continues to catch on is day care for children and elderly who need supervised. It seems that the children learn patience and the elderly are hit in their soft spot, remembering their childhoods and memory improves for a while.

For sure and certain, the Amish are well connected from birth to the grave. We've gleaned so much from the Amish, that when my son at fourteen said Jim was his best friend, my heart soared. Jim was our next door neighbor and seventy. Long talks and lots of lemonade on the front porch made my son learned the values of the Greatest Generation, the ones who lived through the Great Depression and World War II. My son is now thirty-two and he says Jim changed his life. He's never said that about a childhood friend. Maybe it's because the elderly can teach us so much.

Day 17
Turn off the TV

When I thought Miriam Hershberger was a deprived teenager, no television and so excited to go seven miles with me to Randolph New York to a craft store, I just blurted out, "Miriam, what in the world do you do without television? Don't you feel deprived?"

Miriam looked at the white doves that swooped around her barn. "Well, we like to visit. I have lots of girlfriends, and we get together at least once a week to make some kind of craft."

My heart sunk. Friends? I'd seen large groups of Amish women on front porches, just sitting and talking. I, on the other hand, had four kids that I homeschooled and was out four nights a week to violin, piano, karate, and dance lessons. Yep, each child had their own talent and a night that took me away from doing things with friends. Actually, I only had a few close friends at church.

"Do you have lots of friends, Susan?" I asked.

"*Jah*, and so many cousins, I keep losing track of the number. Then there's nieces and nephews…"

My family lived in the Greater Pittsburgh Area, and I longed to live near them. But my husband's job was in New York and we made the best of it.

"So, Miriam, what else besides friends?"

"I love to read. I read a lot."

Another touchy spot. I love to read too, and took a book and read a few pages while waiting for one of my kids to finish a lesson.

"And we spend lots of time as a family…"

Okay, Miriam was hitting a real nerve now. Being away so much at night, I rarely saw my husband. He worked seventy hours a week…but we caught up on the weekends, I kept telling myself. But it wasn't true. Our marriage was wilting due to lack of water and sunshine, just like a plant.

Miriam looked at me in pity. "I can show you lots of other things we do. Work frolics are fun."

I told her I had to run…the clock was ticking and the babysitter needed paid. She took her bags and told me to come back anytime to chat. She wasn't busy.

On the ride home, something snapped in me. Our lives were revolving around two things; our kids and television. My elderly neighbors tried to tell me my kids could all take piano or…maybe nothing. When they were kids, there was no such thing as a private lesson.

So, I talked to my husband, and he smiled so much, I thought he was going to scream, "Touchdown!" Someone had finally gotten through to me that my kids wouldn't die if they didn't have lessons. Our kids wouldn't die if we actually put our relationship first instead of them.

So we pulled the plug on the television and canceled lessons. The kids didn't even mind, saying they'd have more free time. They weren't as addicted to the television as I was, because I didn't let them "waste their lives" watching it. I went cold turkey and it was hard. But I started to see my day was suddenly much longer. I had time to read and visit friends. I got more involved in our church, and volunteered to help with the teens. Tim and I got out our guitars and sang together again.

A year later, I saw a television on in a waiting room at the doctor's office. I just gawked. It was so corny. So unrealistic. So hyped up. It didn't portray real life at all. I knew that, because I actually now had one!

My kids are now in their twenties and thank me for limiting television and not having any electronic games when they were young. They have so many good childhood memories that are real, not living their lives through someone else. That's how the Amish view television. They wonder why people watch other people live, but don't live themselves.

I'm so grateful for Miriam and the wake-up call I got the day we went shopping. My husband and I are so happily married, since we "water" our relationship often because... we don't watch television. We have a television and a DVD library, but it's hardly ever on. We're too busy living.

Day 18
Less choices, less anxiety

I was listening to a sermon the other day, and something struck me deeply. I white-knuckling *every* decision *every* day. Big decisions bring stress, and if you make them daily, you will have no peace or simplicity of mind...

And then I thought of Suzanne Woods Fishers' book, *Amish Peace*. The lacks of choices', Suzanne says, make the Amish not deprived, but free to not have to make so many decisions.

To understand this, I'd like to share a letter to my four adult "kids" to help them recognize that they inherited a white-knuckle mind from their father and yours truly.

Dear kids,

Dad and I have been talking lately. We both tend to make life changing decisions daily, and know that it's brought stress into our lives, and for me, unsettling dreams. Just over the past week, we talked about the following:

Should we go on vacation this year or not?

Should we get a Lab, a poodle or a Labradoodle?

Should we keep savings in dollars or invest in assets?

Should we buy the little house for sale down the road (an asset) to rent out as an investment?

Should we start another business? We can buy Amish rockers off of Roman at wholesale and sale them online? It would help Roman and is a tax right-off.

We're both making this the 'Year of Health and Fitness'. Should we buy a rowing machine? Join Weight Watchers online or go into town for meetings?

So many people are hurting and I can't keep up with making prayer shawls. Should I start a knitting circle, since more hands make light work?

Should we join a small group Bible study in our church?

Should we start a small group Bible study in our house?

Should we build a little cabin in our woods in Smicksburg, or get a retro trailer off Craigslist? If we build a tiny house cabin on wheels we pay no taxes and give employment to Melvin and Levi, our Amish friends.

Should we go to visit family in Italy this year, and if so, should I write about my awesome Italian grandma as a memoir?

Should we get a goat this year or expand our herd of chickens? Or get a cow? If we get a cow, we'll need a pole barn, and that means employment for Amish friends.

We got a letter asking if they could do fragging on our fifteen acres in Smicksburg, which is on the Marcellus Shale. I threw the letter in the garbage, since it would upset the Amish who border our property. No, it bothers me that they'd would go in and cut down virgin trees. Am I anti-fragging or not? Do I want this country energy sufficient?

These aren't even all the things we discussed, as some are private. So, over the past weekend, we went out for our 32nd wedding anniversary, and when we caught ourselves making "big decisions" we changed the subject. I cannot believe the peace this action produced. As you know, Dad and I love the Amish and are drawn to their culture, but is it the lack of decisions they have to make every day that we envy, in a good way? Time will tell, as we've decided to take time once a week or month to talk about big or troubling decisions. We suggest you all do the same...

Love you more,

Mom

Day 19

Be true to yourself

Author Bronnie Ware, in her book, *The Top Five Regrets of the Dying,* made headlines when, gasp, one of these regrets was:

"I wish I'd had the courage to live a life true to myself, not the life others expected of me."

That is shocking! The Amish can teach us much in this area. I have yet to meet an Amish person with a life full of regrets. They were free to leave the community when young, contrary to popular belief. An elderly woman, nearly ninety years old, told me with tears in her eyes, that when she looks back over her life, she's ever so happy to be raised Amish.

The pull towards the Amish is a phenomenon, and I wonder if it's because they can put the "pause" on life and think about what kind of life they want to live. Their occupations are more varied than you might think. Our friend, Noah, moved his young family to New York to be a farmer. He simply said, "Well, I've always wanted to be a farmer." Plain and simple, just like that, he moved away with the blessing of the community, because they said, "Yep, Noah's wanted to be a farmer since a wee one.

Noah is not just drifting through life, but has courage to live intentionally. He has the courage to live a life true to himself.

Now, my confession. I was a career driven woman. Having my elementary education and psychology degree, I felt like a fish out of water in the 1980's being a stay at home mom. I loved my kids but the "mass mind" of society said I was ruining my life by not working. Mentally I was caving in, but my heart was in my home. I loved being a mom of four preschoolers in a decade that said I was irresponsible for having so many children. Didn't I know the average parents in the USA only had two kids? Didn't I know what a daycare center is?

Here's what happened. I faced the 'mass mind', a psyche term that just means "what everybody else is doing", and thought about how I wanted to look back over my life. Then I prayed and asked the Lord to give me strength to live it out. We ended up homeschooling for twenty years. (I am not saying putting your kids in school is wrong, but for us, homeschooling worked) Now in my 50's, I look back and shudder to think what my life would have been if I hadn't put on the brakes and *gained the courage to live the life true to myself.*

The Amish in New York helped me tremendously to feel normal as a stay at home mom. And on one income, my hubby and I began homesteading, "puttin' up" food to last us through the winter. We were tight, very tight, but we learned many lessons from our Amish friends on frugality, and found it so much fun to find a deal (and extra money in the bank), we were then led to get involved with giving to a charity in Haiti. Living among the Amish also led me into a great knowledge of the Amish culture, and who would have known how popular they would be today and anyone would want to read about them in my books?

Day 20
Live without electricity for a day

I've always wondered if I could live without electricity, like the Amish. Well, we lost our power for three days due to a thunderstorm: three *long* days. Yes, the days seemed lengthened without electricity. Time slowed down...as well as my mind. After we got batteries for our flashlights and candles, Tim and I looked at each other? *Now what?* But our son and daughter-in-law soon knocked on the back door, asking how we were (they now live in back of us). We soon started chatting longer than usual. It reminded me of the Walton's, and it was simply charming.

After an hour, they went back to their place. Tim and I read a lot at night, but we looked at each other: *Our Kindles are dead!* Did we have to read the old-fashioned way? Turning pages in a book is so...cumbersome. But I got out my Jan Karon book I'd been meaning to read, and by candlelight started *In the Company of Others: A Father Tim Novel.* Karon helps us celebrate the simple things in life, so the book starts out with Father Tim and his wife Cynthia arriving at an inn in Ireland, and the power is off due to a storm. *How ironic!* They read by candlelight and talked into the night, relishing time together.

Karon always helps me see the charm in everyday life. So I looked for it over the next few days, as we lived without electricity. Without the distraction of the internet, I closed my eyes to listen to the many birds at my birdfeeders. But I heard cows! I told my husband, and he said with a cocked eyebrow "There's cows down the road…" I'd never heard them before. I see them all the time, but was thrilled to hear them moo. Then a rustling sound, a clanking. No way! I could always here the train whistle two miles away, but the boxcars? That was baffling because I love farm country *and* railroads, and to think that over the past fifteen years I'd missed the sound of cows and the railroad. Tim said he hadn't noticed how loud the crickets were. I hadn't noticed them at all.

These past three days helped us see that living without power makes time stand still, and who doesn't want more time?

Day 21
Write handwritten letters

It's the number one question readers ask: "Can you get me an Amish pen pal?" I think it's nostalgia, many missing the days of a letter you can touch, smell, feel. A letter that someone took the time (which is precious) to sit down and write, maybe on fancy stationery. And what if it's a love letter? My Aunt Anna got letters regularly from her fiancé during World War II. What about letters written home from summer camp or college? Are they all endangered?

As the Amish take us back to a simpler time, when running to the mailbox was a treat to see if some surprise was in store, I've been trying to slow down and write letters. I have to say, my once A+ Peterson Method of Handwriting (what I was taught in elementary school) is most likely a C- now but I'm aiming to improve. Why? Well, I find it really relaxing. Many studies in mental health show that too much high tech and not enough high touch is robbing us of peace.

So if handwriting is something that connects us to others and helps us process our emotions, as some claim, I've started to do this on a small scale, sending small notes of encouragement. When I say *small*, I mean *small* stationery. Maybe something you can write a few paragraphs on. This doesn't make me feel like I'll get writer's cramp or that I'm not saying enough. I also have a female Amish pen pal and then letters are written to Amish friends who may only live half an hour away. (With no phones, you have to write)

I will answer the question on how to get an Amish pen pal. It's my "cut and paste" answer that I give when asked.

Visit an Amish settlement and make an initial contact by asking for a recipe. Amish women love to share their recipes! This is a good way to make an Amish friend, and then perhaps, you can write to each other. To find the nearest Amish settlement near you, visit <u>www.amishamerica.com</u> . At the top left corner is a tab called "Amish State Guide". Click on your state and see the nearest settlement.

Day 22
Gain a sense of accomplishment through hard work

It never ceases to amaze me how the Amish treat their young teens like grown-ups. It reminds me of other cultures where boys are considered men at the age of thirteen. Some of you may chuckle at that, thinking of an immature middle school teen right now. But is the immaturity of some teens the American culture's fault?

My dad left his home at fifteen to join the CC Camps during the Great Depression to send money home to his mother and other siblings. When I see pictures of him in New Mexico building roads, he looks like a man. When I visit Amish settlements scattered across Western Pennsylvania, I see young teens driving huge hay wagons. I know a few of them aren't even teenagers. Their self-worth is so much higher than *English* youth, it sometimes takes me back. If parents aren't home when visiting a family business, a young son or daughter will come out and explain the business and clinch a sale. It amazes me.

One Amish family I know, depends a bit on the income of their oldest daughter, who's the local schoolteacher at sixteen. The whole family of twelve works at the vegetable stand, greenhouse, make crafts, just about anything to pitch in. When I see this young teacher, I think of my mom. She did the same thing as a youth. My grandma was a seamstress, and my mom did embroidery or other fabric arts to embellish dresses. I see this all the time in Amish country; mothers and daughters working on something to sell, whether a craft or jams, fudge, pies, or other edible delights.

I got my certification as a Montessori preschool teacher, and the approach to training children is similar to the Amish. As soon as a child can do something for themselves, or for the group, they're required to do it. So, if a child can push a broom, they can sweep. It's almost comical to see little three year olds with their pint-sized brooms clean-up after an activity. Cleanup is a part of the program. But I see this in Amish families all the time.

Getting back to teenagers, I really believe that as soon as they're able to work, or contribute, it makes them feel needed and important, and less self-centered. When I see rebellion in a teenager, I wonder if he/she doesn't feel needed. Everyone wants to feel like a part of something bigger than themselves.

Day 23
Take a walk

How many steps per day are enough to keep you trim and prevent obesity? A pedometer study of an Old Order Amish community showed that their average man logged 18,000 steps per day and their average woman logged 14,000 steps per day, and they had one of the lowest rates of overweight and obesity of any community in North America.

The only day their average dipped as low as 10,000 steps was on Sunday, their "day of rest".

When visiting my cousins in Italy, I stopped one day, and said, "I cannot walk anymore." My cousin, ten years my senior, made fun of me. "Bambina," he chuckled. "No crying." You Americans no walk!!!

The Amish walk a lot and when you stop by to pick them up, asking if they need a ride, they scratch their heads. "Only live fifteen farms down." Or they may be walking with friends and family and say they're just out for a stroll. They're not so distracted by technology and enjoy nature more than most folks.

Besides health benefits, walking helps clear out the cobwebs in the mind. When a kid, my mom used to say, "Go outside for a while and let those cobwebs be cleared out of your mind." Being a very visual person, I took it as an insult. Was my mind dirty, needing cleaned? As I grew up, I knew the meaning and benefits. Charles Dickens said, "'Walk and be happy, walk and be healthy." Most of his long treks across London freed his mind to imagine many of the characters and plots that made him such a literary genius. Writing helps the dust settle or be blown out. (Not that there's dust in my brain). The fresh air and oxygen intake makes for good mental health.

Some experts say being outside for 20 minutes a day will make you happier. I tried it last autumn during my 'putting up' harvest season. I spent little time inside and I felt like a kid. I know my Vitamin D was boosted, but there's just something about being outside, walking around the garden and our hobby farm that took me back. Trees dripping with apples took me back to picking fruit and berries with my elderly neighbor when a child. C. S. Lewis says "When I became a man I put away childish things, including the fear of childishness and the desire to be very grown up." Taking a stroll or walking around the property I don't feel very grown up, and kids who romp around are thinner and healthier, too.

Day 24
Get a sense of humor

When Noah showed up to work on our addition, he came loaded with a joke for the day. He'd tell it to other Amish workers and we all had a laugh. Humor is a part of their culture. They tease each other and have odd nicknames, like Short Laughing Martin. And they collect tongue in cheek proverbs like:

Every family tree has a little sap.

Kissing wears out, cooking don't.

Always do right. This will gratify some and astonish the rest.

There are some Amish that can double me over laughing, but Ida has the corner on it. She wrote a letter that made me laugh, fret, then giggle, and then back to laughing. She starts out with:

Here I am finally answering your letter! Isn't this just terrible? I'm very sorry and hope you will forgive me? (She inserted a funny looking smiley faces with huge eyes)

She has a paragraph of small talk about her husband and twelve children, but then goes right into shopping:

Today I go to Punxsy to buy groceries. I pay a taxi to take me, wish you'd be the one taking me, I haven't forgotten our shopping trip! (Really big eyes in smiley face) I love auctions, flea markets and yard sales. If we go to town, we stop at every garage sale we see. Saturday, (a week ago) we went to Blairsville to that big Flea Market and it was so much fun! Now I'd like to go to _____ of course, now I can't think of the name but it's up there near Spartensburg. I do a lot of my Christmas shopping like that since I have twelve kids, other friends and relatives. It can get very expensive so I'm always watching my money.

Then she went on to tell me about her quilts:

Mom sent for more batting, but it felt too soft to handle etc. I was very disappointed in it cuz you can't make fine even stitches, and hopefully the lady that owns the quilt isn't fussy. (Here she has a big frowning mouth).

The problem with the batting was that they got a bad batch. It happens, but they had a deadline on this one quilt. All her quilts are

65

exquisite. But she went on to say how hard it is to sell quilts now etc. and other personal things. She was actually fretting, and asking me advice on where to sell. Then she reminds me that she still doesn't have a copy of my book *Knit Together* that I promised to drop off at the store, seeming a tad bit ticked off, since it's been over two months since I gave my word…hint, hint…but then she lightens right up again:

My garden is doing pretty good. We have radishes, onions, some early tomatoes, squash & lettuce. I have all this stuff in my garden because I want to lose some this unwanted fat! (BIG FROWNING FACE HERE) *I went on a 3-week diet and lost 20 lbs. which I was very pleased, but now I want to lose another 20.*

Ida is an herbalist, and she tells me the herbs her family is taking:

I have an order to send out for some herbs and I want to make a ginseng tincture for Joe (her husband) *That's all he'll take. NO PILLS! And I want to make "Malissa Supreme" for the children. It's for their brains. Helps their learning – like school children.*

(She has teenagers who are out of school, since Amish only go to eighth grade, so she's saying her teens' brains need some help...

She ends by saying:

Well here I am still scribbling, but I could go on and on, talking would be so much better! Love and God Bless, Ida.

Ida is a spunky Amish woman and went through a gamut of emotions in this four-page letter, but notice the humor. She really cracks me up. She wants to be a character in one of my books. She said, "Don't use my real name, but you could use Iva...sounds similar."

Day 25
Keep looking forward

I was in quite a slump all weekend. My daughter has Crohn's Disease and though grown and married, I still can't stand to see her go through a flare-up. I cry, even inwardly shake my fist at God. Why? Why so much suffering in one person's life?

So I go through the regular routine of thinking of people who are having a harder time. I thought of my friend with Parkinson's, another with M.S....no relief. Then I thought of loved ones who are struggling with organ transplants, to no avail. No relief. I am a mom hurting because of her daughter's pain.

I was digging quite a cavern of self-pity and anger so deep, I just felt like staying in bed and reading all day today. Believing God always goes before me, making my path straight or more bearable, I thought of what transpired over last week, and I thought of Smiley.

Smiley is an Amish man in his mid-thirties who should be cast in *The Lord of the Rings* as a very merry hobbit. He has a permanent smile etched in his face and laugh-lines around his eyes. What's so inspirational about Smiley is that years ago, he and his wife survived a tragic house fire...some of his children did not. I'm sure he grieved, but now he has a secret glint in his eyes, as if to say, "I know something you don't. I've been through the refiner's fire, and came out as pure gold."

When I first met this awesome young man, I asked him why he was called Smiley. He just said he smiled a lot, he supposed. He was working on putting a new roof on our house, and another Amish fellow pulled me aside and told me Smiley's tragic story. As usual, I have 1001 questions, so I asked how he could still be so merry. Didn't he grieve? Don't the Amish believe in crying? "We move forward, *jah*?" Ray said. I stood there, dumbfounded.

When taking Smiley home later that day, I told him I was so sorry to hear of his loss. Thinking he wouldn't want to talk about it, he surprised me and opened up. He said that he sorely missed his 'first family' but God has given him another one, and he moves on in life.

I saw Smiley last Friday at a fishing hole with three young sons, laughing and having a good time. He has moved on, and today, I will too. My problems are so petty compared to his loss, but the lesson is the same. Keep looking forward, and instead of shaking the fist at God, open it and take His hand.

Day 26
Be thrifty

Before I knew any Amish folks, I had an advantage to thrifty shopping, since my mom and dad were both immigrants. When you see through the eyes of a foreigner. You see the materialism and entitlement mentality that many Americans have. As my Italian grandma used to say if I wanted something expensive, "Hey *Kad*, you think *you-a something-a* special, *uh?*"

When I had four kids under the age of seven living in rural Upstate New York, I met many Amish, and became close with Harry and Katie Hershberger. He had a variety store attached to his house, being wheelchair bound, and we shopped there regularly. What struck me right off the bat was there was no pressure whatsoever from Harry to buy something. This is so simple, but hard to live by. We're always bombarded with advertisements, but the Amish pay in cash, and know a penny only goes so far.

One day, after picking Katie's brain for cost effective recipes, she mentioned their food co-op. It was an "Amish only" *closed* bulk store. Instead of showing a card to get in, I was to say, "Harry and Katie sent me." I'll never forget our first visit. I had all four kids in tow, and we walked into the store behind an Amish house, and all eyes landed on us, full of suspicion. "Harry and Katie sent me," I quickly said, and with relaxed faces and smiles, they welcomed us in. You see, a co-op is a lot of work for a few people, to benefit the Amish community. I didn't contribute to their communal way of living and was about to reap its benefits, but that's how much a real friendship with an Amish family is valued. I learned later we were called "Trusted English Friends."

Back to shopping. My jaw dropped when I saw all the prices in this co-op. C-H-E-A-P. The Amish don't believe in price gouging, but helping each other save. The women in the store give out cost saving recipes. The Amish collect these recipes, and try other ways of making it better with less money, as if it were an art form. My favorite to this day is making granola. The Amish put in everything edible but the kitchen hand pump, mix in gooey brown sugar syrup, and consume it. "The kids don't know there's stale cereal in there," they'd say. Well, I tried it, and it works.

So, the Amish work hard to help each other save money, and we can do the same. When I see an item majorly on sale, I text people in my 'co-op' and ask if they need any. When I go up to Smicksburg to Lydia's dry good store, I contact my 'co-op' and buy for them. They do the same, when they see a sale.

If you ever want to see animated Amish people, go to a rural Wal-Mart! It's so fun to watch them. They don't go often, maybe once a month, but do they ever stock-up. There's a bus from Smicksburg, PA to Indiana, PA, fifteen miles away. I was at Lydia's after one of her Wal-Mart sprees, and she and her husband were lit up and very animated. "Do you know how cheap it is to get walnuts at Wal-Mart?" they asked with glee, skipping around the kitchen, putting their groceries away. I had to hold back the laughter. The Amish really think it's fun to save money.

Fun to save? Why? Like I said, when you pay cash for everything, you know there's a limit, right? So, it's almost like a game to them as to how much they can get with their dollars. I think there's a real joy in a goal that's met, too.

One thing that may shock you is that the Amish also attend garage sales, flea markets, second-hand stores and auctions. I saw a group of Amish women at my local Salvation Army. Of course, they weren't buying clothes, but books to devour or household items, such as dishes, pots and pans. Many people wouldn't be caught dead in a Goodwill or Salvation Army, but not me. I learned early in life from my Italian grandma, "I'm not *something-a* too special." And since we pay cash now, too, I get really excited to see how I can stretch a dollar.

Day 27
Slow down & keep in pace with nature

When you drive through most Amish settlements, you'll see massive front porches with chairs and benches. If you ride around after dinner, you'll see Amish folks seated there and no one is working. No one staring into a bowl of peas that need shelling. Men aren't out there with their tools trying to fix something. No, they are looking at each other, communicating. In a day of text messages begging for our every beck and call, it's sad that this is a nostalgic thing: people sitting on their front porches, sipping lemonade and talking. Face to face.

On one of my many trips to Smicksburg, I drove by an Amish friend's house, and saw her little family on the front porch making ice cream. I didn't want to intrude, but they earnestly waved for me to come join them. So I did and I'll never forget it. The family was yapping up a storm, and I joined in. They commented on birds seen at their hummingbird feeder that hung nearby, the peeper frogs that sang a deafening song in their nearby pond…just small talk.

When I got home, I did a little experiment. What if I sat on my front porch and just relaxed? It could be a refuge from daily concerns, a little haven. So after dinner, Tim and I sat on our little portico for a little while, and noticed things we hadn't before. The red-tailed hawk that lives in the meadow across the street was being chased by crows. Hummingbirds sucked nectar from our rhododendron bush in blossom. Then we saw something that slowly appeared after the drizzle subsided. A rainbow. We would have missed it if we had been looking down at laptops and cell phones.

Once again, the Amish make me reevaluate my life, and Tim and I now use our front porch often.

Day 28
Learn Amish 'rules'

The Amish treasure rules, but not the kind you may think. All the "thou shalt not" rules are not so typical of their culture as you may think. Yes, there are many things not to do, but many things *to do*.

A little book, *Rules of a Godly Life,* is found in most Amish and Mennonite homes. It has three basic sections. Rules on thoughts, words and works. They are proverbs of sorts, which help steer a Christian in the right direction, similar to the book of Proverbs in the Bible, though they are not weighed as heavy as the latter.

I started to read Rules for a Godly Life and was so impressed. I include many of the proverbs in my books, and I hear from readers on how much they've gotten out of the profound little truths.

I break them down into bite size pieces and then meditate on it. Here's the first part of Rule I and what I got from it.

Awake in the morning with your thoughts turned to God…

How can I awake with my thoughts turned to God if I've just been chased in my dreams all night by giant spiders? Or haunted by painful memories?

In Psalm 5, we see King David's call for help and I take comfort that he struggled in the morning, too. In verse one he asks God *to give ear to him.* In modern language, he's asking God to listen to him. In the next verse he asks God to *"Hearken unto the voice of my cry"*. He then goes on to say that he will pray in the morning...

My voice shalt thou hear in the morning, O LORD; in the morning will I direct my prayer unto thee, and will look up.

Psalm 5:4 translated from the Hebrew is:

O LORD, in the morning shalt Thou hear my voice; in the morning will I order my prayer unto Thee, and will look forward.

The original Hebrew really strikes me. It's saying that David talked to God in the morning, and then looked forward, as opposed to looking backwards.

Day 29
Celebrate

The woman I use as the character of Granny Weaver in my novels told me how she and her sisters celebrate birthdays. "Well, it all starts with a surprise," she quipped, her light blue eyes twinkling. "On the day of a sibling's birthday, we celebrate, give our loved ones a present, but we don't tell them who it's from."

"What?" I gasped. "How do they know who to thank?"

"We all get together in October, or whichever month suits us, and we celebrate Sister Day. On that day we all guess who gave the presents."

I was too stunned to talk. Some Amish women have several sisters and that would mean they'd have to remember not only what they got, but what they gave. I'm trying to think what I gave my sisters for their birthdays last year! I have two!

"It's another way to get together," Granny said with a gleam. "It's lots of fun and keeps us connected."

Amish children have birthday parties that take me back to my youth in the 1960s. Levi's little girl had ten boys and girls running around a water pump when I stopped in to see his father. Oh, that camera of mine makes me sin! I took a few snaps, knowing I'd Photoshop their faces out, but I got busted and had to delete them. But these children were having fun, the old-fashioned way, like we used to run through the water sprinkler all day with neighborhood kids. Times were simpler.

Well, anyhow, someone called out that it was time for cake and the kids went charging towards the house cheering. I've never seen this level of excitement over having a cake before. Levi told me that his wife made a big cake. "The *kinner* love cake and ice cream!"

Oh, once again, I was six years old with friends, balloons and a party dress waiting for my mom to bring out her homemade cake with "cooked icing", my favorite.

Day 30
Choral singing

"Music is my life," was my mantra in high school, so starting college as a music major was a no-brainer. When I met my voice teacher, I was so embarrassed for him. He was an extreme stutterer; but when he sang, he was instantly cured. Oh, he was so inspirational. Research suggests there's a brain overlap with music and speech. Music also has the ability to help dementia patients remember. Music is the last thing to decline in the brain. As a beginning music therapy major, I was floored.

Here's a snippet of Kimberly Sena Moore Ph. D in Psychology Today's article *Memory through Choir?*

"Let's take choir, for instance. Think about some of the benefits that come from singing in a choir—there's deep breathing involved (respiratory strength), vocalization (speech production), the need to focus on a given task (sustained attention), the challenge of learning new material (learning and memory), the pleasure derived from performing (emotional benefits, like pride), all within the context of a social group (socialization)."

Pretty impressive, huh? What most don't realize is that singing is a staple of Amish culture. Singing at home, church, Singings (for youth to meet up) or singing in three-part harmony while working on our barn. It was the most heart-warming look into Amish comradery; I soaked in the beautiful German accapella (no harmonica in tow), closing my eyes and fantasizing once again that I was on the set of *Little House on the Prairie.*

And then I thought of the joy my kids brought to nursing homes as we tried to be the Von Trapp Family Singers. Patients were wheeled in or used their walkers to get to the lounge room. Tim and I strummed the guitars to slow songs like *Kumbaya* or *Amazing Grace.* After a few songs, the audience was so excited, they shouted out, "Play something faster." So we did and some stood and others clapped their hands. The room was filled with laughter and joy and comradery. To be honest, I didn't want to expose my kids, then four years old to nine, to the nursing home environment. But after that night, we went back faithfully once a month and my kids learned some valuable lessons from World War II Vets.

A benefit music plays in the Amish church services is the ability to connect with the writers of their hymn book, The *Ausbund.* The core of it is fifty-one songs written by Anabaptists while imprisoned between 1535 und 1540 because of their convictions. Some didn't survive and many were martyred. A fresh respect for their ancestors and the courage to keep the faith, solidifies their beliefs.

I find this wonderful. C. S. Lewis said that every century has their faults and is shortsighted… "It is a good rule after reading a new book, never to allow yourself another new one till you have read an old one in between." So, to sing like the Amish, throw in some old tunes.

Day 31
Don't be a people pleaser
You can tell when you're on the right track. It's usually uphill.

My journey living among the Amish started when I was in my late 20's, living in rural Upstate New York. A neighbor came by to ask me if I wanted to join her in her "ministry" to the Amish. She said she took crates of oranges to the settlements so they wouldn't get scurvy. "They don't know anything about nutrition and don't eat fruit and lack Vitamin C." Well, I wanted to help these poor uneducated backward folks. So I agreed to go with her, but she forgot to buy oranges, and said we'd just visit families to see if they were okay. Well, we did, and I came home with a recipe for granola, rich in dried fruits that are loaded with Vitamin C. I was so taken with these kind people, maybe because my expectations were so low. This woman, who had a 'ministry' to the Amish, never went back with me. She thought I got my brains sucked out, being lured in by "those people who don't bathe". Hmm. I guess beauty is in the eye of the beholder, because I was hooked! (And, yes, the Amish bathe!)

It was the 1980's, and the Amish weren't glamorized like they are today. I became friends with many Amish families in the Cherry Creek area ten years before Beverly Lewis helped to accurately portray their culture in her books. For 10 years I saw so much prejudice against the Amish it sickened me. Here's a list of what people thought in the 80's about the Amish:

- Amish can't read and are uneducated
- Amish children are beaten with horsewhips to join church
- Amish don't brush their teeth or bathe or use deodorant
- Amish poach deer and other wildlife and don't get hunting permits
- Amish don't pay taxes
- Amish women are abused, having to stay home and raise their children.
- Amish don't talk to "outsiders" (non-Amish)

This list could be a mile long. When such comments were made, I asked, "Have you ever met an Amish person?" Many said, "No way. They're a cult." Oh, I would get so angry, knowing otherwise, and I defended them, which only fed into people's imagination that I too was backwards like them because I home-schooled *and* was a stay-at-home mom.

Well, fast-forward 30-some years. Now the Amish are glamorized in many romance novels or demonized in "reality" shows. I confess, I can be preachy, standing up on my soapbox. I feel like James Fennimore Cooper, author of *Last of the Mohicans,* writing for his children what Native Americans were really like. Several years ago, I started writing to preserve stories about Amish culture for my children. I didn't want my kids to forget about our Amish friends, Harry and Katie, and how the community cared for this Amish family who was hit hard by tragedy. I wanted them to not forget the reasons I had courage to home-school and be a stay-at home mom was inspired by the Amish culture that put family first. I want my grown kids to pass on to their children that the Amish are not a cult, *but a different culture.*

Culture is defined as "the customary beliefs, social forms, and material traits of a racial, religious, or social group" (Merriam-Webster) I get a different cultural experience when chatting with the Amish, much like my Italian cousins who live in rural Italy, or when talking to Haitians on a mission trip. They have a different culture, and I glean so much from listening to them, it shifts my thinking for the better.

If you don't have a Bible, I've included the *Sermon on the Mount,* a staple in Amish thinking. I've discovered that If you read it, you will be blessed and less stressed...

Sermon on the Mount ~Matthew 5 -7

World English Bible

The World English Bible (also known as the WEB) is a free updated revision of the American Standard Version (1901).

Chapter 5

[1]Seeing the multitudes, he went up onto the mountain. When he had sat down, his disciples came to him. [2] He opened his mouth and taught them, saying,

[3] "Blessed are the poor in spirit,
for theirs is the Kingdom of Heaven.
[4] Blessed are those who mourn,
for they shall be comforted.
[5] Blessed are the gentle,
for they shall inherit the earth.
[6] Blessed are those who hunger and thirst after righteousness,
for they shall be filled.
[7] Blessed are the merciful,
for they shall obtain mercy.

[8] Blessed are the pure in heart,
  for they shall see God.
[9] Blessed are the peacemakers,
  for they shall be called children of God.
[10] Blessed are those who have been persecuted for righteousness' sake,
  for theirs is the Kingdom of Heaven.

[11] "Blessed are you when people reproach you, persecute you, and say all kinds of evil against you falsely, for my sake. [12] Rejoice, and be exceedingly glad, for great is your reward in heaven. For that is how they persecuted the prophets who were before you.

[13] "You are the salt of the earth, but if the salt has lost its flavor, with what will it be salted? It is then good for nothing, but to be cast out and trodden under the feet of men. [14] You are the light of the world. A city located on a hill can't be hidden. [15] Neither do you light a lamp, and put it under a measuring basket, but on a stand; and it shines to all who are in the house. [16] Even so, let your light shine before men; that they may see your good works, and glorify your Father who is in heaven.

[17] "Don't think that I came to destroy the law or the prophets. I didn't come to destroy, but to fulfill. [18] For most certainly, I tell you, until

heaven and earth pass away, not even one smallest letter or one tiny pen stroke shall in any way pass away from the law, until all things are accomplished. [19] Whoever, therefore, shall break one of these least commandments, and teach others to do so, shall be called least in the Kingdom of Heaven; but whoever shall do and teach them shall be called great in the Kingdom of Heaven. [20] For I tell you that unless your righteousness exceeds that of the scribes and Pharisees, there is no way you will enter into the Kingdom of Heaven.

[21] "You have heard that it was said to the ancient ones, 'You shall not murder;' and 'Whoever murders will be in danger of the judgment.'[22] But I tell you, that everyone who is angry with his brother without a cause will be in danger of the judgment; and whoever says to his brother, 'Raca!' will be in danger of the council; and whoever says, 'You fool!' will be in danger of the fire of Gehenna.

[23] "If therefore you are offering your gift at the altar, and there remember that your brother has anything against you, [24] leave your gift there before the altar, and go your way. First be reconciled to your brother, and then

come and offer your gift. ²⁵ Agree with your adversary quickly, while you are with him on the way; lest perhaps the prosecutor deliver you to the judge, and the judge deliver you to the officer, and you be cast into prison. ²⁶ Most certainly I tell you, you shall by no means get out of there, until you have paid the last penny.

²⁷ "You have heard that it was said, 'You shall not commit adultery;' ²⁸ but I tell you that everyone who gazes at a woman to lust after her has committed adultery with her already in his heart. ²⁹ If your right eye causes you to stumble, pluck it out and throw it away from you. For it is more profitable for you that one of your members should perish, than for your whole body to be cast into Gehenna. ³⁰ If your right hand causes you to stumble, cut it off, and throw it away from you. For it is more profitable for you that one of your members should perish, than for your whole body to be cast into Gehenna.

³¹ "It was also said, 'Whoever shall put away his wife, let him give her a writing of divorce,' ³² but I tell you that whoever puts away his wife, except for the cause of sexual immorality, makes her an adulteress; and

whoever marries her when she is put away commits adultery.

³³ "Again you have heard that it was said to them of old time, 'You shall not make false vows, but shall perform to the Lord your vows,' ³⁴ but I tell you, don't swear at all: neither by heaven, for it is the throne of God; ³⁵ nor by the earth, for it is the footstool of his feet; nor by Jerusalem, for it is the city of the great King. ³⁶ Neither shall you swear by your head, for you can't make one hair white or black. ³⁷ But let your 'Yes' be 'Yes' and your 'No' be 'No.' Whatever is more than these is of the evil one.

³⁸ "You have heard that it was said, 'An eye for an eye, and a tooth for a tooth.' ³⁹ But I tell you, don't resist him who is evil; but whoever strikes you on your right cheek, turn to him the other also. ⁴⁰ If anyone sues you to take away your coat, let him have your cloak also. ⁴¹ Whoever compels you to go one mile, go with him two. ⁴² Give to him who asks you, and don't turn away him who desires to borrow from you.

⁴³ "You have heard that it was said, 'You shall love your neighbor and hate your enemy.' ⁴⁴ But I tell you, love your enemies,

bless those who curse you, do good to those who hate you, and pray for those who mistreat you and persecute you, [45] that you may be children of your Father who is in heaven. For he makes his sun to rise on the evil and the good, and sends rain on the just and the unjust. [46] For if you love those who love you, what reward do you have? Don't even the tax collectors do the same? [47] If you only greet your friends, what more do you do than others? Don't even the tax collectors do the same? [48] Therefore you shall be perfect, just as your Father in heaven is perfect.

Chapter 6

"Be careful that you don't do your charitable giving before men, to be seen by them, or else you have no reward from your Father who is in heaven. [2] Therefore when you do merciful deeds, don't sound a trumpet before yourself, as the hypocrites do in the synagogues and in the streets, that they may get glory from men. Most certainly I tell you, they have received their reward. [3] But when you do merciful deeds, don't let your left hand know what your right hand does, [4] so that your merciful deeds may be in secret, then your Father who sees in secret will reward you openly.

⁵ "When you pray, you shall not be as the hypocrites, for they love to stand and pray in the synagogues and in the corners of the streets, that they may be seen by men. Most certainly, I tell you, they have received their reward. ⁶ But you, when you pray, enter into your inner room, and having shut your door, pray to your Father who is in secret, and your Father who sees in secret will reward you openly. ⁷ In praying, don't use vain repetitions, as the Gentiles do; for they think that they will be heard for their much speaking. ⁸ Therefore don't be like them, for your Father knows what things you need, before you ask him. ⁹ Pray like this: 'Our Father in heaven, may your name be kept holy. ¹⁰ Let your Kingdom come. Let your will be done, as in heaven, so on earth. ¹¹ Give us today our daily bread. ¹² Forgive us our debts, as we also forgive our debtors.¹³ Bring us not into temptation, but deliver us from the evil one. For yours is the Kingdom, the power, and the glory forever. Amen.

¹⁴ "For if you forgive men their trespasses, your heavenly Father will also forgive you. ¹⁵ But if you don't forgive men their trespasses, neither will your Father forgive your trespasses.

[16] "Moreover when you fast, don't be like the hypocrites, with sad faces. For they disfigure their faces, that they may be seen by men to be fasting. Most certainly I tell you, they have received their reward. [17] But you, when you fast, anoint your head, and wash your face; [18] so that you are not seen by men to be fasting, but by your Father who is in secret, and your Father, who sees in secret, will reward you.

[19] "Don't lay-up treasures for yourselves on the earth, where moth and rust consume, and where thieves break through and steal; [20] but lay up for yourselves treasures in heaven, where neither moth nor rust consume, and where thieves don't break through and steal; [21] for where your treasure is, there your heart will be also.

[22] "The lamp of the body is the eye. If therefore your eye is sound, your whole body will be full of light. [23] But if your eye is evil, your whole body will be full of darkness. If therefore the light that is in you is darkness, how great is the darkness!

[24] "No one can serve two masters, for either he will hate the one and love the other; or else he will be devoted to one and despise the

other. You can't serve both God and Mammon. ²⁵ Therefore I tell you, don't be anxious for your life: what you will eat, or what you will drink; nor yet for your body, what you will wear. Isn't life more than food, and the body more than clothing? ²⁶ See the birds of the sky, that they don't sow, neither do they reap, nor gather into barns. Your heavenly Father feeds them. Aren't you of much more value than they?

²⁷ "Which of you, by being anxious, can add one moment to his lifespan? ²⁸ Why are you anxious about clothing? Consider the lilies of the field, how they grow. They don't toil, neither do they spin, ²⁹ yet I tell you that even Solomon in all his glory was not dressed like one of these. ³⁰ But if God so clothes the grass of the field, which today exists, and tomorrow is thrown into the oven, won't he much more clothe you, you of little faith?

³¹ "Therefore don't be anxious, saying, 'What will we eat?', 'What will we drink?' or, 'With what will we be clothed?' ³² For the Gentiles seek after all these things; for your heavenly Father knows that you need all these things. ³³ But seek first God's Kingdom, and his righteousness; and all these things will be

given to you as well. ³⁴ Therefore don't be anxious for tomorrow, for tomorrow will be anxious for itself. Each day's own evil is sufficient.

Chapter 7

"Don't judge, so that you won't be judged. ² For with whatever judgment you judge, you will be judged; and with whatever measure you measure, it will be measured to you. ³ Why do you see the speck that is in your brother's eye, but don't consider the beam that is in your own eye? ⁴ Or how will you tell your brother, 'Let me remove the speck from your eye;' and behold, the beam is in your own eye? ⁵ You hypocrite! First remove the beam out of your own eye, and then you can see clearly to remove the speck out of your brother's eye.

⁶ "Don't give that which is holy to the dogs, neither throw your pearls before the pigs, lest perhaps they trample them under their feet, and turn and tear you to pieces.

⁷ "Ask, and it will be given you. Seek, and you will find. Knock, and it will be opened for you. ⁸ For everyone who asks receives. He who seeks finds. To him who knocks it will be

opened. [9] Or who is there among you, who, if his son asks him for bread, will give him a stone? [10] Or if he asks for a fish, who will give him a serpent? [11] If you then, being evil, know how to give good gifts to your children, how much more will your Father who is in heaven give good things to those who ask him! [12] Therefore whatever you desire for men to do to you, you shall also do to them; for this is the law and the prophets.

[13] "Enter in by the narrow gate; for wide is the gate and broad is the way that leads to destruction, and many are those who enter in by it. [14] How narrow is the gate, and restricted is the way that leads to life! Few are those who find it.

[15] "Beware of false prophets, who come to you in sheep's clothing, but inwardly are ravening wolves. [16] By their fruits you will know them. Do you gather grapes from thorns, or figs from thistles? [17] Even so, every good tree produces good fruit; but the corrupt tree produces evil fruit. [18] A good tree can't produce evil fruit, neither can a corrupt tree produce good fruit. [19] Every tree that doesn't grow good fruit is cut down, and thrown into the fire. [20] Therefore by their fruits you will

know them.[21] Not everyone who says to me, 'Lord, Lord,' will enter into the Kingdom of Heaven; but he who does the will of my Father who is in heaven.[22] Many will tell me in that day, 'Lord, Lord, didn't we prophesy in your name, in your name cast out demons, and in your name do many mighty works?' [23] Then I will tell them, 'I never knew you. Depart from me, you who work iniquity.'

[24] "Everyone therefore who hears these words of mine, and does them, I will liken him to a wise man, who built his house on a rock. [25] The rain came down, the floods came, and the winds blew, and beat on that house; and it didn't fall, for it was founded on the rock. [26] Everyone who hears these words of mine, and doesn't do them will be like a foolish man, who built his house on the sand. [27] The rain came down, the floods came, and the winds blew, and beat on that house; and it fell—and great was its fall."

[28] When Jesus had finished saying these things, the multitudes were astonished at his teaching, [29] for he taught them with authority, and not like the scribes.

Rules of a Godly Life seemed so intimidating, I almost didn't buy it. *Who wants more rules or restrictions?* But what I discovered was that these rules were more like boundaries, guideposts, or fences so you don't get off track and end up in a muddy cow patch.

Rules of a Godly Life

Part I

Thoughts

(Translated by Joseph Stoll from the German "Regeln eines Gottseligen Lebens," as found in the First Part of "Geistliches Lust-Gartlein Frommer Seelen.")

Beloved friend, if you desire to live a holy and God-pleasing life, and to inherit a home in heaven after this life, then you must bring ALL of your life, all your thoughts, words, and actions into subjection to the teachings of the Bible, as God has commanded. Deut. 5: 32, 33. This is your only Rulebook of Faith. King David wrote, "I thought on my ways, and turned my feet unto thy testimonies" (Ps. 119:59), as much as to say -- "I regard and examine all my thoughts, words, and deeds, to see if they are according to thy commands; so that, perchance, if I have erred or wandered from some truth, I may return to the right."

First of all, let us consider our THOUGHTS. Take the following rules seriously to heart:

1. Awake in the morning with your thoughts turned to God. Think, this might be your last day of life. And when you go to bed at night, pause a moment to realize that it is unknown to you whether you will awake again on this earth, or whether your next awakening may be at the resurrection. For this reason, we can see that it is expedient to pray daily; in the morning and again at evening, come before God upon your knees, thanking Him for continued care, confessing your sins and shortcomings, and praying for forgiveness.

2. Keep free from wicked, idle, or unclean thoughts. Prov. 4.23. For as your thoughts are so is your speech, your conduct, and your entire way of life.

3. Think often on the four last things: on death -- there is nothing of which we are more sure; on the Judgment Day -- there is nothing more terrible; on hell -- there is

nothing more unbearable; and on heaven -- there is nothing more joyful. He who thinks on these things will shun much sin and will be diligent in the way of salvation.

4. On the Sabbath especially take note of the wonderful works of God; of the creation and governing of the world, and of our Redemption. Make the Sabbath a day of prayer, of listening to and studying sermons; make it a day of holy thoughts and holy conversation. In this way you can keep the Sabbath holy, as is so often commanded in God's Word. If one does not keep the Sabbath holy it is certain that he will also take into contempt all the other commandments of God.

5. In everything you do, ponder well before you start what the outcome may be. Think, would you be willing to be found doing what you plan to do should you be called that hour by death, to appear before God? Never allow yourself to become involved in anything which destroys your hope and assurance of salvation. Live each day as if it were your last.

6. If anyone wrongs you, exercise a forgiving spirit and patiently dismiss the matter. For if you take the wrong to heart and become

angry, you hurt no one but yourself and only do what your enemy wants you to do. If, however, you patiently forgive him, God will in His own good time judge the evildoer and bring your innocence to light.

7. Beware especially of an uncontented and rebellious spirit. Actually it is through the will and grace of God that you suffer and are troubled. God has blessed you with unnumbered gifts to supply your needs, and likewise for your own good has meted out of trouble and pain that you may remain humble. In the midst of trouble remember that you through your sinfulness deserve much greater punishment.

8. If other people praise you, humble yourself. But do not praise yourself or boast, for that is the way of fools who seek vain praise. Be honest in all your dealings and this will be enough reward; then others will praise you.

9. Be not overly concerned in another man's business, and what is of no concern to you, avoid.

10. In tribulation be patient and humble yourself under the mighty hand of God, with these thoughts foremost in your mind: first,

that it is God who chasteneth; second, it is for your good; third, God will ease the burden; fourth, He will give you strength to endure; fifth, He will deliver from affliction at an expedient time.

11. Never consider any sin as small or of no account, because every sin, though it seem ever so small, is a transgression against God. A small sin that is loved and nurtured can condemn a man as well as a gross sin. A small leak, if not repaired, can sink a ship in time; likewise a small sin if continued without repentance can sink a soul and send it to hell. Beware, then, not only of great sins but also of small. Make a habit of overcoming every small temptation, and you can be master over great ones, too. Especially shun willful sinning, that ye provoke not God to anger; for a truth it is hard to obtain forgiveness for sins that were willfully committed.

12. "Rejoice not when your enemy falleth" (Prov. 24:17). What happens to another today may happen to you tomorrow, and he who rejoices at the calamities of another shall not go unpunished. Prov. 17:5.

13. Permit not envy or hatred in your heart, nor carry a grudge against anyone. God loved

us when we were His enemies and therefore He expects us to love our enemies for His sake. It is but a small thing for us to forgive our enemies, in comparison to what God has forgiven us. Even though you may think your enemy unworthy of your forgiveness, it is well worth doing it for Christ's sake.

14. Do not think any less of a godly and holy life because it is held in contempt by the unsaved. For the same reason, do not forget the gravity of sin just because it is so widespread and most people live a sinful life. Righteousness and the majority are not always on the same side. The way to hell is always full of wandering souls. Matt. 7:13. If God should ask you on the Judgment Day, "Why did you desecrate the Sabbath? Why did you indulge in drunkenness? Why were you dishonest? Why did you pass your time in hating and jealousies?" Would you then answer, "Lord, I did so because almost everyone else did so."? This will be of all answers the least worthy, and God will say, "Because you have sinned with the majority, you will go to hell with the majority."

15. If you have an important decision to make, or you find yourself in circumstances

where you know not what is best to do or answer, spend at least one night in meditation. You will not be sorry.

16. Never go to sleep without considering how you have spent the day just past, what you accomplished for good or evil, and you will readily perceive whether you are using your time -- fleeting, unredeemable time -- in a constructive manner or not.

Part II

Words

1. Think! For every idle word you speak you must give account thereof in the day of judgment. Matt. 12:36. "In the multitude of words there wanteth not sin" (Prov. 10:19). Seek to avoid, therefore, all non-edifying talk; let your words be thoughtful, few, and true. Consider beforehand if what you are about to say is worth saying. Practice saying much with few words. Never present a tale as true unless you know for certain that it is so; it is better to say nothing at all than to say something that may turn out to be false or otherwise of no value.

For once it becomes known that you are not conscientious to always speak only the truth, no one will believe you even when you do speak the truth. If, however, you have great respect for the truth your every word will carry more weight than those spoken under oath by a liar.

2. If you desire in honorable company to be joyful take care that your merriment prove worthy of Christian love, purity, and respectability. Avoid, therefore, rude insults, mocking speech, indecent words, and filthy jokes of which respectable people would be ashamed. First, because lewd conversation of this sort is outward proof of an unregenerate heart; "For out of the abundance of the heart the mouth speaketh" (Matt. 12:34). Second, because smutty humor and immodest words smooth the road to dishonorable deeds.

Yet you may say, "One must have something to say when in company with his friends to pass the time and to delight each other." This is indeed a wretched excuse. Such mirth is clearly forbidden by God's Word, "Neither filthiness, nor foolish talking, nor jesting, which are not convenient," says the Apostle Paul, are to be permitted. "For because of these things cometh the wrath of God upon the children of disobedience" (Eph. 5:4, 6). Through such evil talk and vain mirth the Holy Spirit of God is grieved. Eph. 4:29-30.

The tongue is the glory of man and the honor of the body. Shall it then be misused in unwholesome speech? When the tongue becomes corrupt it defileth the whole body, filling it with unrighteousness. See James 3:6. Loath all filthiness; let your speech be always full of love and to the edification of those who hear you, that they may be strengthened thereby. Use the gift of speech as a means of rebuking the idle, of instructing the ignorant, and of comforting the troubled. God will reward you with a fuller measure of His gifts. See Mark 4:25.

3. Be especially diligent to keep free from the vulgar thoughtless habit of swearing and the profane use of the holy name of God. It is indisputable evidence of a frivolous, impious, and ungodly character. It is also true that he who seeks with oaths to add strength and truth to his words is seldom a man of integrity; for if he has no scruples against misusing God's name, why should one suppose that he has any conscience against

107

lying? "But let your communication be, Yea, yea; Nay, nay: for whatsoever is more than these cometh of evil" (Matt. 5:37). And that you might the better avoid profaneness, seek not the companionship of the profane, where you, too, may through familiarity fall into the habit. Rebuke a friend for profaneness, if he accepts it; if not, there is no gain in rebuking. See Proverbs 9:8.

4. Be not too ready to believe everything you hear, and do not repeat everything you hear, lest in this way you lose a friend and gain an enemy. When you hear complaint or gossip about another, thoroughly investigate the actual circumstances before offering your criticism or passing your opinion.

5. Confide to no one your personal secrets unless you have beforehand found him to be worthy of your trust. Here is one way to prove him and learn to know him well: confide to him some secret of small importance; if he keeps it to himself it is an indication of his trustworthiness. However, it is not wise to inform any friend carelessly of all your secrets. There is a possibility that at some later time you may have sharp

differences and then he may use his knowledge to your harm.

6. Do not speak evil of friends; rather, speak well of them wherein they deserve praise. What is not praiseworthy keep to yourself. Slanderings and scornful gossip are poison to any friendship. If you are present when others speak disrespectfully of one who is absent, search first your own heart before joining in; without doubt you will find there the same (or greater) shortcomings. This should move you to better yourself, and yet keep you from speaking evil of others and belittling them.

7. When you need advice do not seek a counselor on the basis of his prestige or esteem among the people. Go to those who have experience in that concerning which you seek counsel. For if a man accustomed to recognition above his fellows gives you advice, and you do not comply with his recommendations because you feel they are impractical for you, he may be insulted and become your enemy.

8. If someone with good intentions gives you advice which turns out to be not good, do not hold it against him. For even a good counsel sometimes fails, and there is no one on earth

who can tell what the future holds. No one is wise enough or has foresight enough to do so. Do not scoff at the advice of unaccomplished brethren who have your welfare at heart.

9. Do not make fun of another's weaknesses. Instead, think of your own shortcomings. Gal. 6. We all have our weak points, and there is none of whom others say not, "O that this or that were different." Either we are, or have been, or may become subject to most anything, even as others. Therefore show patience and sympathy toward your brother's weaknesses and mistakes. At the same time, do not strengthen him in sin by your nonchalance or by neglecting brotherly admonitions and reproof. If you wish to admonish a brother be careful to bring your reproof at a suitable time; for a reproof at the wrong time may easily do more harm than good, especially if the rebuke is too sharp or not tempered with gentleness. A reproof is like a salad; it needs more oil than vinegar.

10. Make a habit of not discussing or judging another's words unless you know you have heard and understood aright what they meant to say.

11. You cannot have disputes and divisions with fellow humans and still have peace with God. If you love God, you must also love your fellow men, because God has commanded it.

12. Patiently bear your cross without complaining; for your adversary may rejoice at your discomfiture, and others will think less of you.

13. Consider him a friend who rebukes you privately. It is a pitiful state-of-affairs indeed, for a man to have no one who dares to correct him when he has need of it. For such a man is likely to think he makes no mistakes if he receives no reproof, and will live on in error to his own destruction. Whereas, this might be prevented by an earnest appeal from a friend.

Everyone most certainly needs instruction at times. The eye sees all and seeks the improvement of all, but it cannot see itself to aid its own improvement. Thus it is with us -- we are so prejudiced in our own favor that we cannot see our own mistakes and shortcomings as easily as those of others. Therefore, it is very necessary that we have their help, since they can see our needs much more clearly than we ourselves can. Regardless whether reproof is given justly or unjustly, whether it comes from a friend or an enemy, it can do a wise and understanding person no harm; for if it be well-grounded it is a reminder to better himself, and if it be false it can serve as a warning of what to shun. If you are a person who can not bear reproof, your only choice is to never to anything wrong.

Part III

Works

1. Do no evil, even if it is in they power to do so. Do nothing in secret of which you would need to be ashamed before men. Remember with Joseph that, though no man sees, God sees all; and that your conscience will testify against you. Abhor all sins, not alone those that are apparent to others, but also secret sins. For even as God is a righteous God, so will He, if you do not repent, bring all your hidden sins to light. I Cor. 4:5; Ps. 50:21.

2. Stand firm, with all your strength, against your bosom sins, those which your personal nature, more than any other sin, has a tendency to commit. One man loves the

honor of men; another has a love for money; a third may tend to drunkenness; a fourth to the sins of the flesh; a fifth to pride, etc. Against your strongest evil inclinations you must above all others defend yourself, for if you overcome them you can easily master other temptations. AS a fowler retains control of bird by one leg, so has Satan that man in his power who succumbs to one temptation, and this as fully as if he fell to all.

3. If you desire to avoid sin you will need to shun every occasion and opportunity that tends to evil-doing. He who does not avoid the conditions that lead to evil can not expect to overcome sin. Evil companions lead to sin, such as those from whom one hears indecent speech, by which he may easily be misled and corrupted. Bad company ruins good morals. I Cor. 15:33. Evil associations are the Devil's drag-net, with which he draws many to perdition. Avoid companionship with ungodly, lewd persons. "If sinners entice you, do not consent" (Prov. 1:10, RSV). Those who spend much time with sinful companions are easily corrupted by them, adopting their habits of speech and becoming similar in character ere they realize it. Evil companions demand conformity. In their company one

must either sin or suffer scorn. With this in mind a devout man avoids the company of the wicked. If you do not wish to be enticed to fornication and impurity, flee diligently from occasions and persons where the door to these sins would be open. To escape drunkenness (which is the broad way to hell), seek not the comradeship of a drunkard, and look not to him as a friend. For of what help is such a friend who may ruin your life, yea destroy your salvation? For experience teaches that more people are killed by friends by way of drunkenness than are slain by the swords of enemies. More people have perished by wine than have been drowned in water. Beware of all allurements to sin! You know not how soon you may be ensnared by Satan and sin.

4. When you are tempted by others or by your own impulse, to do harm to a fellowman, pause to consider how you would feel if others did so to you. Do nothing to others that you would not wish them to do to you. "All things whatsoever ye would that men should do to you, do ye even so to them." Matt. 7:12. What you yourself dislike do not to others ...

5. When you in your calling face a great undertaking, do not lose faith in the power of God to provide. Begin nothing without first praying for God's blessing, for without His sanction all our cares and labors are in vain. Ps. 127:1-2. On the blessings of God depend all things. Pray the Lord to bless your labors, and then proceed to the task at hand with joyful spirit, committing all to the wise providence of God, who cares for us and supplies the needs of those who fear Him.

6. Do not attempt supporting yourself in any occupation forbidden by God. For to what advantage is wealth won at the expense of your soul? Matt. 16:26. Even though you may make great temporal gains through dishonesty, you will thereby forfeit the blessing of a clear conscience. Who can bear the burden of a disturbed, nagging conscience? Be diligent, therefore, as was the Apostle Paul, always taking pains to have a clear conscience towards God and towards men. Acts 24:16.

7. Do not be proud and overbearing because you have been blessed with this world's goods, or with outstanding personality features; for God who has given can also take

away, and may do so if you through pride or contempt of others make misuse of His gifts to you. Even though you possess certain qualities of which you may feel proud, they are more than offset by your many bad habits and shortcomings which prove you unworthy in your own eyes. He who knows himself well is certain to find enough of human frailty to make it extremely difficult for him to consider himself better than others.

8. Be a true servant to Christ, not only by attending church services or by taking part in religious ceremonies, but throughout every area of your life, shunning all sin, and with a true obedient spirit obeying all the commandments of God. Be not satisfied with a reputation for godliness: let your character be equally good. Woe unto the man who is not pious yet wants to be considered as such.

9. Do not think that it will suffice to only serve God yourself, and not see to it that all in your care do likewise. The duty of every father lies not alone in personal service to God, but also in influencing his family and servants to do likewise. God has commanded, "And these words, which I command thee this day, shall be in thine heart: and thou shalt teach them

diligently unto they children, and shalt talk of them when thou sittest in thine house, and when thou walkest by the way, and when thou liest down, and when thou risest up." Deut. 6:6, 7. So did Joshua, the gallant God-fearing hero, informing the people of Israel that whether or not they served the Lord, he and his house would do so. Josh. 24:15. A father is as accountable for the welfare of those in his house as a government for her charge or a pastor for his flock. He must therefore be deeply concerned that his entire household truly worship and serve God, which is the only way for them to obtain salvation.

10. Detest idleness as a pillow of Satan and a cause of all sorts of wickedness, and be diligent in your appointed tasks that you be not found idle. Satan has great power over the idle, to lead them into many sins. King David was idle on the rooftop of his house when he fell into adultery. II Sam. 11:2-5.

11. Practice modesty in the wearing of clothes, and have nothing to do with pomp and luxury in raiment. It is great vanity to spend as much on one suit as would ordinarily be required to clothe two or three persons. When you become old and think back to the

time when you sought to adorn yourself, you will feel only regret that you once loved such vain display. Read much in God's Word and you will find many warnings against pride. No other sin was punished more severely. Pride changed angels to devils. A once powerful king, Nebuchadnezzar, was transformed into a brute beast to eat grass like an ox. And Jezebel (a dominant queen) was eaten of dogs as the result of her pride. II Kings 9:30-37.

12. Do nothing in anger but consider well before you act, lest you be sorry later and will acquire a name of evil repute. In time your anger will cool and you will be able to decide wisely what has to be done. Make a difference between one who has wronged you against his will through lack of forethought, and one who has deliberately and maliciously done so. Be gracious to the former and let your reactions toward the latter be tempered with righteousness.

13. Be not too intimate with any man, except he fear God; for it is certain that any and all friendships, however established, built on any other foundation than the fear of God, may not last long.

14. For the sake of their friendship it is best for friends not to become too confidential; for this life is so filled with change and circumstances that it is hard for any man to retain the good will of all his friends unto the end of his days.

15. If you chance to fall into any kind of dispute with a friend, do not despise him for this reason, nor betray his confidences. Prov. 11:13. In this way you may win him again as a friend.

16. No one is his own master, only a steward of that which is in his care. Therefore give of your goods to the poor and needy, wisely, willingly, and heartily. 12:13; II Cor. 9:7.

17. Preside over those in your charge with kindness and meekness, rather than to subject them to fear and terror... The righteousness of God can not long endure tyranny; an oppressor does not rule long. An overly severe administration of justice is gross unrighteousness. God requires meekness and humility of those in authority as well as justice. Therefore govern your subjects with love and mercy, so that they will love you more than fear you.

119

18. Finally, be friendly to all and a burden to no one. Live holy before God; before yourself, moderately; before your neighbors, honestly. Let your life be modest and reserved, your manner courteous, your admonitions friendly, your forgiveness willing, your promises true, your speech wise, and share gladly the bounties you receive.

ABOUT THE AUTHOR

Karen Anna Vogel writes stories that take readers into a real life situation where they can learn to solve their problems in a Biblical manner or by the Amish philosophy of life.

Karen has worn many bonnets: stay-at-home mom to four kids, home school vet, substitute teacher, wife to Tim for 35 years, Christian counselor.

After her kids flew the coop, she delved into writing, and many books later, she's passionate about portraying the Amish and small town life in a realistic way, many of her novels based on true stories. Living in rural Pennsylvania, she writes about all the beauty around her: rolling hills, farmland, the sound of buggy wheels.

She's a graduate from Seton Hill University (Psychology & Elementary Education) and Andersonville Theological Seminary (Masters in Biblical Counseling). In her spare time she enjoys knitting, photography, homesteading, and chitchatting with family, friends and readers.

The best place to connect with Karen is at her author page on Facebook at: www.facebook.com/VogelReaders.

Or, at her author page

www.karenannavogel.com/contact.

Karen Anna Vogel Book List

Smicksburg Tales Series

Amish Knitting Circle: Smicksburg Tales 1

Amish Knitting Circle: Smicksburg Tales 2

Amish Knit Lit Circle: Smicksburg Tales 3

Amish Knit & Stitch Circle: Smicksburg Tales 4

Amish Knit & Crochet Circle: Smicksburg Tales 5

Amish Herb Shop Series

The Herbalist's Daughter Trilogy

The Herbalist's Son Trilogy

Standalone Novels

Knit Together: Amish Knitting Novel

The Amish Doll: Amish Knitting Novel

Plain Jane: A Punxsutawney Amish Novel: Bronte Inspired

Amish Knitting Circle Christmas: Granny & Jeb's Love Story

Amish Pen Pals: Rachael's Confession

Christmas Union: Quaker Abolitionist of Chester County, PA

Love Came Down at Christmas: A Fancy Amish Smicksburg Tale

Nonfiction

A Simple Christmas the Amish Way: Inspiration from Amish Friends to Escape the Holiday Chaos and Enjoy the Season (Amish Cookie Recipes Included)

Printed in Great Britain
by Amazon